C000227084

Room of Thieves

ANGELA CLELAND was born in Inverness in 1977 and grew up in Dingwall by the Cromarty Firth. She studied English Language and Literature at the University of Glasgow and in 2003 completed an MA in Creative and Life Writing at Goldsmiths College, London. In 2006 she won the Templar Poetry Pamphlet and Collection Competition and published her pamphlet *Waiting to Burn* and her full collection *And in Here, the Menagerie* as a result. *Room of Thieves* is her second collection.

ALSO BY ANGELA CLELAND

POETRY
And in Here, The Menagerie (Templar Poetry, 2007)

PAMPHLETS
Waiting to Burn (Templar Poetry, 2006)

Room of
Thieves

by

ANGELA CLELAND

SALT

CROMER

PUBLISHED BY SALT
12 Norwich Road, Cromer, Norfolk NR27 0AX
All rights reserved

Salt Publishing 2013

Printed in the UK by TJ International Ltd, Padstow, Cornwall

Typeset in Paperback 9 / 13

ISBN 978 1 907773 51 8 hardback

1 3 5 7 9 8 6 4 2

for Granny

Contents

Acknowledgements

Some of these poems first appeared in the publications *Long Poem Magazine, Mslexia, The North* and *Smiths Knoll*. 'The Second Fall of the Eagle Stone' first appeared online at The Poet's Letter. 'Emma's Porch' was commended in the Bridport Prize 2010 and appeared in that year's anthology. 'Yana Phuyu' was commended in the Mslexia Poetry Competition 2011. 'My Hands are Slippery' first appeared in *Entailing Happiness,* a volume celebrating Robert Vas Dias' 80th birthday.

Thank you to everyone who has offered me support and criticism over the past few years: Robert Vas Dias and his small group seminar; Roddy Lumsden and his Wednesday group; Michael Laskey, Peter Sansom and everyone who accompanied me on the Advanced Poetry Seminar in 2010. Special thanks goes to my husband Matthew for continuing to find time to discuss poems with me over a glass of wine despite the demands of having two young sons and actually being more interested in aeroplanes.

Brinacory

Island we could not land on. Island that would wreck us
if we tried, far down the loch past the glamorous
shadow of Black Crag.

No kinship betrayed with the other island gangs:
their spillage formations, their bays loose and soft as inner arms,
their sand as pale.

Distilled, pure island, dense and domed as a plug of moss
kicked from a giant's wall. About it, black rocks
rose in a ring

at a sliver of beach, the earth's petrified viscera, its broken folds.
I longed to scramble over them, cut my bare soles
and lose my clothes to them.

Brinacory, the other islands would never have known to be jealous
while, with our boat in broken bark pieces
on your barricade,

we tacked between your besom-close trees, weaving their loom
with our feral bodies, on all fours, eyes wide in the gloom,
growing large as goose eggs.

As we pass I keep you to the grey edge of sight. If these oars
lift now, they will never stroke again; your shores
look almost possible to me.

Blaeberries!

I cry out, as if I've never seen them before
growing wild on this island. I pinch one

between finger and thumb; velvet
rubs away to reveal its colour.

Her voice comes in pieces through the trees
from the beach – *don't eat that!*

The men have been going back there to –
I let it fall from my hand, small blue

rabbit dropping. Later, searching
for pine cones up on the island's temples,

out of sight, I find they are everywhere,
dizziness spots, pea-sized, dust-blue,

looking cheeky in the undergrowth –
here, where only I have come,

where surely no-one ever came
to go. I gather a palmful, burst them

between my teeth: the neat pop
of skin, the grit of seeds, the sweetness

of small islands. Dad calls us
back to the boat, those fish are out there

somewhere. I take three bracken-bound steps,
stop, feel a sudden need

arrive like a tang in the throat, rise up
like a small boy's thumb to his nose.

Elasaid

It is the early 1800s. Young Dugald MacDonald leaves his home at Meoble by Loch Morar to fight in the Peninsular Wars, leaving behind his deerhound.

I

On days you could have walked on the loch,
on days it would have swallowed you whole,
days of glass, days of pitch and all days in between
I watched for your return, monument on the flat rock.
Your goodbye had been different this time –
the scratch at the neck too long,
the palms of your hands too firm at my temples,
holding my head while my body wagged.

The women were small and grey in your absence,
never looked to the bay. From time to time a boat came
and every boat put ashore a man – you
until his feet touched land. Man disguised as man.
My tail would drop its tentative greeting, rest
in a shivering curl. He'd have your posture, your way
of squinting at the hills, perhaps your hair,
but nothing more. Without turning their heads,
the women grew smaller, greyer.

II

I took to the hills. You had slipped by me as I slept,
you must have. Damn me for sleeping.
In the hills above the loch, you were everywhere:
at our fishing spot the tree kept your scent,
the rock held the warmth of your flesh;
your swears and whistles, at first as close
as the breeze, grew lost in the long grass,
drew miles ahead of me. You were nowhere.

I hunted you in motes. My stealth set fires
in the dumb buttonhole eyes of the sheep.
The burn that had rolled a soft quenching song
in your presence bared its rocks, held the tang
of a carcass upstream. I spent the days sniffing
your trail cold. And when the scent was gone
I licked the rocks, the leaves and earth
to revive it, until my nose and tongue
were raw and all I could taste was myself.

III

Master can you forgive me the hot advances
of the wolf, forgive me my giving in?
At the bay the women greeted me with paleness,
with a haunted eye and withdrawn hands.
The itch at my scruff grew gluttonous as a tick
until only his teeth were sharp enough
to scratch it. When he tracked me I was sick.
I was sick of myself. But you should know

I used him that day just as he used me
and all it was was weight and warmth.
In those hills where everything ran from me,
he didn't. I knew his thirst for pursuit,
knew it would be quenched with the catching.
He knew what to do, knew well
how to do it and for the short spell
we were locked together I forgot you. Forgive me,
for afterwards, I remembered you.

IV

My low-slung belly announced my infidelity,
its hairs standing straight out as if in fright.
The women caught wind of the wolf's touch
and closed the barn doors to me. The lochan
was far enough from the bay, its island
the perfect nursery: brush clad cloud land,
nothing to contend with for its blue wildness.
You knew it well. It used to make you stare.

We always seemed to come home this way
whatever the path we set out on.
Its unearthly darkness had gripped us both:
bottomless well, strange forest at night.
It was only a short swim from shore.
I had tried to get you to follow and though
one time you pulled off your shirt, threw
your skin scent on the wind, kicked off
your shoes and stood, hair scruffed, your eyes
lit with the thought of it, you had never risked it.

V

The emptiness I held in my chest
was folded into the holes in their marrow,
the space inside each splitting cell.
They were as full of emptiness as the sky
and each emptiness wrapped in a film
of what the wolf had given them.
No surprise that they arrived at night,
blind and hungry. They weaned fast.

When they'd found their legs I taught them
to stalk their prey. I did it with ears
still full of your whistle, with a nose tuned
to your scent from searching, with eyes
I'd used to adore you, imprinted your image
alongside the heat of the hunt.
I taught them their teeth, the places to bite,
to grip till the movement stopped, to work
as a pack, work fast. The hills ran feart.

VI

Sometimes I tell myself that the man on the shore
was not you. It was not your call, not your flesh
that emerged dripping from the lochan,
dulled with ice. You must have been cold
as a corpse when you stepped ashore.
I ran to you fast, pups yelping behind –
I'd taught them prey; they'd never known a man –
and I leapt to meet you, your height on hind legs.

Your hands went to my sides as if to wrestle me,
your fingers curled in my coat, I barked
and nuzzled your throat, I felt your head
hard on my neck for a moment before
they piled in to assist the kill.
They took my snaps and snarls for encouragement.
Good pups, they didn't loosen their jaws
until the white pebbles on the beach were pink,
until they each got their share. I taught them this.

VII

I fool myself into thinking that the warmth
I leave where I lie comes not from me,
but from you, up through the ground to comfort me.
I leave your side only to serve your kin.
I exist so close to death I am death
and can feel when one of your blood grows near.
I can see whatever it is that approaches
and will never have my back to danger again.

And they know me, Master, the grey dog of Meoble,
know I have travelled far from the bay
to their flat, this road, their office, their bed
in vain, to stand between them and the end,
substantial as mist and bringing mist's chill,
stopping nothing. And though they know, they call me
old friend, old girl, always reach out a hand
as my name comes to them like a sigh: Elasaid.

NOTES

This poem is based on a version of the story of the grey dog of Meoble told to me
by my mother. She was originally told the story by Sandy MacEachan, known to
the family as Sandy Tougal. Sandy gillied for my Great Grampa Waters on Loch
Morar in the 50s and 60s and when my mother and her siblings went out in the boat
with them, he would tell them folk tales of the loch. The names of the man
and his dog I've borrowed from Mike Dash's article 'The Grey Dog of Meoble',
published in the *Fortean Times* on September 30th 2007.

In the Middle of Loch Morar, Late July

A sewing box
full of fish hooks;
one blue and silver Toby.

Ribbed rubber floor,
wetness bleeding
back and forth.

Dog sniffing
air above water:
a fish hound.

Black depth
and the sky,
broken on ripples.

Clear line
running round itself,
pulled through a noose.

Silver flickering
through fathoms,
sinking out of sight.

Short wooden truncheon,
blood stains:
'the priest'.

[11]

Monster's skin
rolling beneath
reflections.

An afternoon:
sliding droplets
strung out on nylon.

A Big One

Every seventh wave, you said,
and she believed you
to the extent that she still
counts them, attaching
caveats to length of crest,
depth of colour, angle
of approach; making constant
revisions to her rules
for what is and what is not a wave;
patrolling the beach,
offering your fact to each passer by
as if it is a sweet,
eyebrows high in the face of their disbelief.

Tall Thistle Syndrome

The mystery night time beheadings
in the flower fields of Northumberland,
turns out, are the work of a Borders farmer.

He is jealous, says the *Branxton Bugle*,
he has no blooms of his own to match
their Sweet William – do they think
the man is farming sticks up there?

Sure he has flowers. No, you won't see them
from the road, but find a high spot
or take a walk between the tall
seeping stalks – look down.

You'll see where he crouched in their midst
sharpening his secateurs –
waiting for stems that grew too well,
waiting for each drab calloused fist

to split along its feathered seams
and threaten to burst its purple core
to the sky. You'll see how
their withered heads carpet the ground.

And you'll see where, at his field's edge
he paused to oil his blades and where,
without much thought, he gripped them,
climbed the fence and kept on snipping.

The Second Fall of the Eagle Stone

'Coinneach Odhar foretold . . . that Loch Ussie would ooze up through the well and flood the valley below to such an extent that ships could sail up to Strathpeffer and be fastened to the (Eagle Stone); and this would happen after the stone had fallen three times.

'The Eagle Stone has already fallen twice, and on the second occasion the Cromarty Firth flooded up to the old County Buildings in Dingwall.'

(The Prophecies of the Brahan Seer, ALEXANDER MACKENZIE)

Right enough, the stone lay flat,
Pictish eagle remembering the sky,
luck drained from its sculpted horseshoe –
yes, they should have let it lie.

But the council members' socks were wet,
so how could they sniff at the Seer's sign?
They'd fix the Eagle Stone upright
to make sure it stayed cursed this time.

Two held it up, two dug, two ran
to the builders, mixed, and filled the trench,
planned and built a small field round it,
eight foot square with a barbed wire fence.

They drank tea, two by two, in shifts,
each helped to hold the stone up (squint);
when the concrete set, they wiped their hands
and went home. They've not been back since.

Now every night, as they sleep deep,
the concrete cracks a little more,
the Seer turns in his barrel of tar
and the waters swell at the Cromarty's shore.

Yet they believe that they have fixed it
and will not wake till they bash their heads
on their low ceilings one dreich night
when the swollen firth floats up their beds.

The Commission

Fingers and joints, roots and nobbles,
insidious, fast as women's tongues:

the faeries move like the worst kind of insects,
their hissing laughter like wet wood trying
to burn. They are hardened by generations

of men folk bent on levelling their mound,
of blame for stolen livestock, children, brides;
they feed on the thwarted efforts of men.

He should not have fallen asleep on the job,
fallen asleep on their turf, should not
have taken the commission for the damned thing.

Skin hangs on their skeletons like soaked silk,
fleshless mischief. Their stench can be masked,
but never shifted. Now he is moving

among them, feels the texture of wet rock
on his palms, his hands web out before him,
cankerous duck feet. And they are away,

crawling over the stones, unbuilding,
pissing freely as they go, marking their paths
with the scent of bored malevolence.

When he wakes, his palms are split
like scalded tomatoes, dirt buckshotted
into the flesh. The site is rubble

again. He rocks and cries, he knows
they will come every night that he builds.
Only his mother knows how he sleepwalks.

Barn Owl

Your wings were silent, as they always say.
Your progress was soft, round, so butter-smooth

that my eyes followed you idly for a moment
as if you flew with me everywhere.

I breathed the spiralled air from your wake,
saw and ran after you, as if I would join you

where you landed. At the fence I stood and stared
and stared at the trees where you'd most likely landed.

I looked until I realised I'd never find you,
that perched in those bare black branches

you'd be the colour of the sky beyond.
I looked until the blue drained from my eyes.

Two Young Bucks

And there they are, up and already writing my poem,
walking stop motion with hackneyed knees,

spooking each other with an ear flick, an eye white,
kicking up the warning flags of their tails.

They are fickle as children – whatever it was
is forgotten after five sprung bounds, one jumps

at the other as if to say *ha! I am brave,
really*, and the two princes play at kings,

budded heads down and butted tight,
birling in a spray of cool dew,

spiralling closer, young and artless,
winding the morning about them like a fine yarn.

Abduction

Inside, the carriage is panic-plated
red, is stop signals, warning signs, blood
everywhere, danger, danger. This child
is front page news. He's in the hands
of the man sitting opposite, in the hands
of every man in the carriage, trapped
in the jaws of the headline closing around
his school photo. The train brakes scream

and I am back in that ditch at Achilty
straddling the deer's hot ribcage,
hand to its chest, while you try to prise
the dog's teeth free. I hold the deer's head
to mine; I could draw a gut bow across
its cello neck, soft stretch offering
up its quivering strings to the kiss –
I could draw that note again. I don't
know if the blood, wet on your hands,
is the deer's or the dog's or your own.

Tree-broken light flutters through the carriage
as if we are running fast, our hearts are
beating flat out to head-off some beast:
the beast they tell us is coming for our children,
the beast they say has got one, the beast
we have brought with us, the dog
that is running deep and close in the woods.

Frozen Points

We are nasty, cubist, snagging on each others'
angles, grow more acute at each irritation.
The anger of trigonometry frustrated
is sharp in brows, is taut in bodies drawn like bows,
stings along the rims of eyes held open too long
between dry blinks. Our jolting progress, the painful
geometry of upholstery, straight, narrow tracks
beneath, we feel their icy parallelism
with the morning's vanishing form; we could denounce
shapes forever when there

                    above a perfect slant
of fence, simple, a necessary circle of
just-switched-on red: the sun cut neatly from the grey
crowdless sky and we stare. We stare much longer than
we need to, blink and hold its ghost to us, blood-close.

Trackside Semi

Do they know their house
is flowering, its white harled
sepals spread, releasing
a proud-stigmaed bloom,
petals bold and swollen
as burst lips?

Perhaps they do
and are inside troubling
over issues of pollination,
whether it will bear fruit.
They lift their heads at each
distant lawnmower drone,

at the giant insect clatter
of this carriage's wing casings.
They drop their eyes as we pass,
just another train, aware
their house is wearing
their hopes as a buttonhole.

The Suburbs

Everything is disassembled,
reassembled at the other end, this end,
where it is so quiet you can hear
the screws that are loose,
the screws that are missing.

My hands are bruised from allen-keying bolts;
the hairs in my ears tickle with the creak of metal on wood.

A plane flies over

Sleep here is an isolation tank
during the hours forbidden to flight.
I luxuriate in it, open my mouth
for the night to enter
and embalm me wholly.

And how could I never have realised
we owned so many ticking things?

A plane flies over

Your voice is unpolluted,
its frequencies splatter the air,
a Hirstian explosion.
I hear sweet notes that have eluded me
for our eleven years together in cities.

Everything echoes. The air is cold, clear, thin;
zwiebelsuppe, chicken noodle, something Chinese.

                                        A plane flies over

The silence prickles, clean of the sounds
I'd ceased to hear in the city:
people talking on the pavement outside,
yawning upstairs, flushing next door,
vibrating the building around us.

I hold my breath – here is the sound:
the turn of the record before the music starts.

                                        A plane flies over

Here, every creak,
every snap
is set apart
given space
as if this is a Gallery of Fine Noise:

This piece – the creeping stop-cock-cough – how much?
It will sound tremendous in my loft apartment.

A plane flies over, a city passing
through, cancels out everything,
fills in the spaces between sounds
like sand, provides a background
for all other noises to hide; stage
hands dressed in black against
a black backdrop.

Waiting for Connection

I can see it in the air outside, glowing
towers of data, unenterable, unscalable,
a red ghost metropolis risen up
from the frog-squat houses of the suburbs;
stacked to vanishing point, translucent
rooms full of translucent boxes; air
chirruping with information
– I could scoop it hand-over-hand into my mouth,
stick my face in it, holding my eyes
open beneath the surface, roll in it
until my clothes cling to me obscenely.
Its neon walls flyzap possibilities –
to walk down the street, to leave the house –
and anyway all the libraries are shut,
the shops are shut, the houses are shut
and every lit window in their red brick fronts
is a taunting monitor – IKEA, Facebook,
Twitter, IWOOT, Wikipedia,
Amazon, Google, Google, Google . . .
I need connection, I need stuff
and I need it delivered by 9 a.m.
My fingers, oh my fingers are slivered,
my fingers are slivered by catalogue pages,
my mind by the edge of the dead voice
that apologises over and over for the wait.

JAB

SMACK   pop it straight out from your shoulder
SMACK   the line goes your cheekbone – their nose
SMACK   your fist is a pain-in-the-face bird
SMACK   on a spring – let it ping out
SMACK   then back, don't let the other guy guess
SMACK   the time – you don't even need to
SMACK   him hard, just keep him asking
SMACK   close the doors behind it

he is a cuckoo clock with no face   BANG
and you don't know what time it is   BANG
the bird is coming straight out   BANG
again – 4 o'clock, again – 5 –   BANG
at your face from behind its shutters   BANG
how many more times will it   BANG
the heat in your gut is swelling   BANG

SMACK pop it straight out from your shoulder BANG he's a cuckoo clock with no face SMACK the line goes your cheekbone – their nose BANG and you don't know what time it is SMACK your fist is a pain-in-the-face bird BANG the bird is coming straight out SMACK on a spring – let it ping out BANG again – 4 o'clock, again – 5 – SMACK then back, don't let the other guy guess BANG at your face from behind its shutters SMACK the time – you don't even need to BANG how many more times will it SMACK him hard, just keep him asking BANG anger bursts into flame in your gut SMACK close the doors behind it BANG

Cross

Needling of jabs, riddle of ducks and feints,
you wait for a clear target.

It comes, as brief as a spark plug's discharge,
a flash of knicker. You unload

from the pivoting toes of the back leg,
extend through knee, hip, ribs, shoulder, elbow –

you are industrial, a piston, oiled
metal pain. Misjudge

and your attack could be countered,
your nose smacked ice pack absent numb,

worse, your blow could absorb like melt water
into the padding of your opponent's gloves.

Hook

We practise in the kitchen, beat the
crap out of thin air – when I get it right it
hits me: it's the surprising
efficacy of a drunken swipe, it is the door-
slamming motion that
does it, the doll-like softness in the unstrung shoulder
joint, the bent arm pinging round after the body's
twist, the momentum built on a long loose wild swing and the resultant
whiplash, the way that even though the double-visioned fist at first
misses, the elbow never fails to
catch you.

Sparring

Instincts curdle, my nose wrinkles up:
to win, to hit you, to not hurt you.

So many of the blows intended for the face
make contact with air by the right ear, by the left.

To not be so vain as to think I could hurt you,
to not make you want to hurt me back.

So many of the blows we take to the face
must be intended only for air.

Tythe Barn, Bradford-upon-Avon

Was this window intended to be a cross?
It is a sword. He lifts one hand
and lines it up, palm across the white-hot hilt.

Constructing a fifty-one metre long stone barn
to forge just one sword out of light seems mad.
These days, no doubt, there are saner methods.

But then, one wall to serve as mould,
to anchor the stones that harvest the light,
stone for hammer and stone for anvil;

three more walls to hold up the first,
a roof to save the sword from sun damage,
to bring the darkness to temper the blade.

And the fifty-one metres? It is only
by standing a good forty-five back
that the sword becomes small enough for him to hold,

that he becomes large enough to hold it.
Scabbardless, it has been burning a hole
in the air for seven hundred years.

He curls his fingers around the glowing hilt,
like centuries of men before him,
pulls his hand away, a closed fist, empty.

Helen of Sparta

Denied the Krypteia, the coital rush
of the kill, one hot desire
scalds her cheeks, wounds
speckling red through bandage gauze.
It lifts her beauty as a drop of blood
whitens the marble slab.

The fury of three hundred strokes
daily makes her blonde hair
a burnished helmet. Her envies
close rank about her,
a skin of bronze, the tight-packed
scales of the phalanx.

Her ready muscles pull her posture
arrow-straight, goddess-tall;
her eyes flash, oiled blades
turned in light, they bring
a glorious tang to the mouth, iron
death arriving on the soldier's tongue.

When she steps out in her panoply
every man is transfixed
as by an empty pyre, is stiff,
already laid on his shield.
She breathes, fire
in her hoplite heart,

and opens the Hot Gates of her arms
eastward; westward.

Buttons

A scree of buttons in a striped chocolate box
sits on the side by a bundled work shirt.

Through the wall, on the kitchen TV,
news, a woman this time: the footage rolls.

At the blast the buttons start like a flock
from their age-soft box and stick to the air

to be counted and loved one last time:
silver anchor, blue kitten head, ladybird.

All at once an army of ghosts
has ripped open coats, cardigans, frocks

and sent a shrapnel of fastenings hurtling
to wedge in the fabric of five to ten this morning.

Military brass, fake gold, leather,
a stray belt buckle from a favourite dress

are stitched like a poor substitute for stars
to a swollen backdrop of combustion.

Right now this could be any city that has ever been
done up for war. The buttons, medals:

the toggle, the mother of pearl, the shank,
to honour the brave, the young, the late,

the waiting, the happened-to-be-there; the air
is the used-up air of a conscription office.

In the last flicker of the instant – there –
bright in the blaze of the kitchen door,

a factory-made shirt button, white, small,
perfectly round, uniform.

Room of Thieves

She walks into the room,
explodes like a Picasso on its surfaces.
Look there, her button nose amongst the sausage rolls.

Everyone she passes catches something of her.
Her parts are no longer her own:
not that curl turned nearly as an 'o',

not the tilt of her peony head,
not her butterfly eyes, not her warmth
as she pauses at the elbows of conversations.

Look, you would have thought that chap
a gentleman were he not tucking her
pussy bow into his top pocket.

There, the man leaving too early –
is that hamster bulge in his cheek
what you think it is?

Tonight, when the pubs shut, across the city
windows will start with light, blinds
will slide down and shoulders hunch

as if over porn mags, as if trying
to keep a candle lit. And with slight hands,
one will slip an iris from his wallet,

one tip a string of her cold perfume
from the crease of a flier, another
unfold her hand in his like a stray glove.

Back in her flat, removing hairpins,
she'll smooth fingers over where she swears
she'd had a beauty spot, eyelashes, breasts.

One by one, they will turn up,
private things in public places:
her eyes will blink each pause in a pop song,

nostrils raised on canvas will breathe her
through the Tate, seventeen sonnets
will hinge on the fall of her stolen limbs,

her knees will make neat warm hollows
in the latest bestseller (chapter 4, page 53,
the graveside scene).

Three Routes to Immortality

OPTION I: PRESERVATION

She explains why they require the head:
the human soul is a network of fields
thrown up by the coils of the brain
when a simple current is passed through it.
She invokes the ubiquitous geometry of the nautilus,
twirls me like the strings of a double helix
around her little finger. The consulting room
is a soothing fusion of spa and hospital.

There are undeniable diagrams on the wall,
a skeleton strung up like the naked truth.
The complexity of the soul is governed
by the complexity of the brain which generates it:
consider a slug; consider a baby;
think of yourself; consider those first
basic spark plugs firing in the primordial soup.

I nod. I see it, my soul's machine woven
from a single slithery thread at conception
to a grand cathedral of connections, an attic
made rich with time and neglect. I ask
the heaven question. *If there is a god,*
she says, *he's a sparky and heaven is*

the national grid. You're as much yourself there
as electricity is the TV it once powered,
spilling out upon your living room as light.
Better to live on than be homogenised –
but I see you've ticked 'atheist' on your form.

I smile and nod. She's right, the point is moot –
the skeleton grins: *gottle o' geer?*
– and I do not need to be persuaded to live.
I lay my neck on the dotted line.

OPTION II: RECONSTRUCTION

The machine version of my brain is depressingly small.
I was expecting valves and pistons, vast chimneys spewing
pearlescent clouds into the atmosphere;
the claws-on-metal screech and grind of industrial-scale magic,
a bulging midnight warehouse with light escaping at the seams;
warning signs, a trench, at the very least barbed wire.

They say that its size is constrained only
by the width of lines that can be carved onto its surface,
that these days sinister grandeur is small, clean, exact.
And I agree in principle, agree that no, I would not want chimneys
steam-punking my phone. But it feels wrong
that, even these days, I should fit on the tip of my own little finger.

Option III: REPURPOSING

Left arm stretched up, slightly bent, arcing over my head.
Head bowed, neck bared as if to a lover's lips.

The stretch should reach down my left side and the tension pull
my body tight like a carcass on my hand's dead hook.

Right leg extended, feet planted in fourth position
to provide me with elegant balance: think art nouveau lamp.

When the plastination is through they can paint me platinum
and pick out each light-slithered pucker and sinew in gold.

Make sure my right arm is out, palm up and it clutches
an absent glass globe, that my fingers are curled enough that

they will each hold one or two coats; leave a big enough gap
between hand and head for the casual sling of your hat.

Foreign Body

Come closer; she will not wake.

See: as she sleeps, the body is at work
monitoring breath and blood, spinning
dreams to distract her from its process.

It has identified grains of her
tickling awash inside, is carrying them
inwards from its extremities.

Watch at the neck, at the breast, the pulse.

The body's heart rate races with memory
of difference, deep memory always there
but only invoked in the final hours.

Blood cells, fervent carriers,
bring her particles whirling
like silt through veins back to the centre.

There, the pit of rise and fall of breath –

it is here that her grains collect and,
clammed in muscle, compact in a sphere
that grows till every mote is found;

here that through the long hours
the diaphragm, drawn down by brain
and up by air, will turn her, smooth her.

It will not be long till she and the body

part, till she is complete and it
performs its final efficient act:
a cough it knows cannot wake her.

Not long – the dawn shift will find her
on the pillow by parted lips,
a still warm pearl.

What Remains

She has a set of brushes for the small retort,
fine like foal's hair, some straight, some tapered;
even the smoothest bricks
are pockmarked with hiding places.

Her brush strokes are those
of an archaeologist. Delicate, reverential,
her hands flutter as if she is unearthing
the bones of the first child.

Most of what she collects is wood ash.
They leave so little, not old enough
for metal pins, for fillings.
The smallest bones are vaporised.

There is never need of the cremulator.
When she thinks there is a knuckle,
an ankle bone it is dust on her fingertips
before reaching the urn's mouth.

She works each minute as hard as an hour,
is never satisfied, never fails
to crumble at the look in their eyes
at the handing over, at the lightness of it all.

The Extraction Socket

Day one: where it had existed in her,
neat and needed as a tooth: a blood clot
forming; erythrocytes and platelets
trapped in a cat's cradle of fibrin.

Day three: she is replacing the dull throb
at the marginal segment with gummy substitute.
Absence has been overfelt and recedes –
fibroblasts spindle into coagulum.

Day seven: the provisional matrix forms
around a pain now small enough to enjoy.
As she tests her bite, cells
excite with shining leukocytes.

Day fourteen: now and then
she forgets; cell-rich woven bone
extending from the socket wall
ossifies her memory.

Day thirty: she takes a careless bite
and feels the absence of pain in the spot.
In its place, lamellar bone, new marrow,
the surprise of cool apple on gum.

Down

A sharp waxy tube declares itself – pop –
through the tight weave of your cotton top.
You pinch it, as you'd pinch at a skelf,
slide it out through a single thread's breadth,
barbs pulled close, a white, hookless fishing lure.

You take the tweezed curl and cup it in your palm,
trap it in your heartline, smooth your free hand
over the mended fabric of your breast
and feel it: a softness made of a billion
tiny hardnesses, a deep pine forest floor.

Dusk

The chair has no idea. That luxurious creak as I shift in it slowly, lay my head back and open myself to the late afternoon light. The air has no idea, drawing its cool scarf across my arched throat. The bird has no idea as his chest-swelled notes, laudanum, dilate my pupils. The nylon shade has no idea, advancing quietly, it draws my eyes across the close-cut lawn towards the waiting flowers. The fuchsia bud has no idea. It bursts while I am watching, reveals its fleshy frills slow motion. The clouds have no idea. They pull into forbidden shapes, leave a trail of soft noil to absorb the teasing colours of the sky. This dress has no idea, allows the cool hands of the wind to slip through it, move beneath it. Really, no idea. My skin has no idea, as the inside of my wrist slips across my cheek, fingers tease my hairline, track my spine. And as, framed by distance, you stoop and pause, your workings drawn in light and shade, pause as if you will rise holding a golden fruit, as my hand strays like a careless thought to my thigh, you have no idea.

Percussion

He made music on his body.
A cupped hand over the belly
gave a hollow oblong 'fop',
a finger tapped on the button
was more precise: the tight round slap
of a generous raindrop. The more of him
she knew, the more she heard –
different pitches, private rhythms.

It was something in his blood.
She caught, in overheard moments,
his father, his brother drum unawares
a taught refrain, brought man-to-man
down their family tree;
thought there must be a toggle for it
on the Y chromosome, sitting by
eye colour, good taste, chivalry.

After a time, a finger
on his lazy Sunday morning hand
sought out the knot that tied her together,
the knot in the cord that joined her
back to mother, to grandmother;
the never-sagging washing line
that sings of damp bedsheets snapping,
taut enough to twang a tune on.

His finger lifted like a baton,
rested in air, then struck:
plucked out a sound from her navel –
a bright note, new to both.
She heard the pocket of air, like felt,
cushion the blow, tiptoe-gentle;
felt the sound, more oval,
more high-pitched than his.

In days that followed, he found out
more sounds from her, triangular
from her coccyx, sharp popping
from the vales between knuckles,
soft behind knees and beneath breasts,
long, high strips from ankle bones.
He sought notes at each dip, each flexion,
set out to know her score by heart.

and Mrs Smith

In my mind she is always standing on a railway platform,
is holding her hat on in a stiff breeze,
has just walked into a private detective's office,
clutching her gloves.

She wears me like an item
that ought to have gone to charity
long ago. I wear her back
like an invisible fur coat.

She no doubt calls you *darling* in her letters,
darling. I can do it too. *Darling*
call me my new name – it sounds so
filthy – so anonymous!

We are Granny's Pearls

We are held together
by the magnetism of grit,
by skewed gravity, by pressure,
by the pull of big-sister moon.

By the quality of roundness,
by our unique shade of perfumed cream,
by the shape we leave in our silk-lined box.

By the struggle between translucence
and opacity, the attraction
of beautiful objects one to another.

By the tendency to travel single file,
to stand in order of size,
to keep queen bee at the centre,
to come full circle.

By the projected intricacy of the clasp,
by human warmth absorbed and locked
within our cores. By the strength
of very nearly touching.

Sandie Dances

Beneath that blissful private grin
her dance is an elegant shrug
*– hey, maybe I don't even know
you're there* – her eyes look down,
look closed – *maybe
I do* – dips of cool
pool along her collar bone.

She moves, a hanger held up, turned
back and forth to show off
the cut of the cloth;
a cat stretching; a thick liqueur
pouring into itself.

Invisible fingers are scratching
her back, chasing a luxurious itch
up her melting spine.

Her elbows squeeze close-in
to her ribcage, hands and wrists
jutt out – someone
has pinched her cigarette holder
and she hasn't noticed,
doesn't care. Those hands could lift
any moment, say
back off
– I'm not dancing for you.

At the Science Museum

The skeleton of the six-toed cat wasn't where I had promised, but I wanted you to see, so we spent a good two hours looking at things for just long enough to ascertain that they weren't cat skeletons, but not for long enough to see what they were. Anything that wasn't a six-toed cat skeleton, well stuff it. If we'd found it everything would have slid back into place, a cat's worth of bones strung on invisible wires in a super-feline six-toed leap. But we didn't find it; we didn't see it and we didn't see anything else either. Not the Apollo 10 command module, not the history of everything that flies, not the white peacock, not the diving bell, not Difference Engine no. 1. Not the flat face of Stephenson's Rocket, no, not even the bionic eye. Not ourselves remade as men, not ourselves remade symmetrical, not ourselves made fools by the dead, not the basement level where they had engineered a portal to Hell, not his six-toed feline face as it grinned up from the grated pit or the hive of six-toed demons that danced in thrall about their six-toed master.

Emma's Porch

Emma, it is 8 a.m. and the light in the front porch
is the colour of your hair. School is waiting.

The barometer is hanging the top side of fair,
its coils and springs pulling both ways,
teasing the atmosphere like a fine wool.
The tension holds the needle static, so the whole
appears to be broken, as barometers sometimes do.

I touch my nose to it and breathe; imagine it is a silent clock
which does time backwards as well as forwards.

Of course there is hoovering
and conversations high over the hoovering
and the claim of being 'almost ready'.
I am sometimes late to call for you,
you are never ready and there is always hoovering.

I count passing cars, bright paint samplers,
as they bobble the patterned glass of the front door.

Your Granddad's shoes are gone from the coat stand,
there is at least one jacket less and the smell,
well it is the same, but a note has ceased to sound,
like a vital spice missing from a dish.
I think of each of the objects that hangs orphaned in his shed.

I am always waiting in the hallway;
there is no going in with shoes on.

I look behind the upright of the coat stand
for that single foam bead
on the foam bead wallpaper
where I press my thumbnail every morning.

My Hands are Slippery

and this thing is a fingernail-proof tangerine,
a pistachio nut with a too-small opening,
a biscuit tin with a sticking lid,
a stubborn jam jar.

But here you come to distract me,
peel back an edge,
hit it with your shoe,
clamp it in the door frame,
get on your rubber glove and loosen it,
so it just gives.

Good Day in Peru

Learn the syllables:
bway-noss dee-ass.

Now forget enunciation.
Allow your vowels to fall
to the back of your throat.

Defuse your plosives,
let air pervade them, feel
your voice form a fine mousse.

Let the slow breath sighing through
to the front of your palate
dissolve *ess*.

Imagine you have a lazy mouth,
are bored of talking, have just
woken in the evening

with eyes full of sunset,
with a mouthful of honey,
speak through your sleep.

You are ready to lose the whole day,
let it slide unsaid
from your carelessly parted lips:

buenos, buenos, make it soft,
like a long afternoon kiss.

The Harpy Eagle, a Theft

The oxbow lake offers up:
birds, cayman, yellow piranha.
I switch my brain from *giant otter*
to *oh well*. We head back.

On the silt-thick Tambota,
our guide, alive with the sight
of a harpy eagle, sparks the air
with thrilled whispers – *men*
will spend lifetimes

dressed in jungle, crouched in hot
shade, in grass shelters
day on day, for years
and never see one.

My palms sweat
jungle. I unfold binoculars
on their plastic elbow,
lift them to my eyes, a poacher
reaching into a Fabergé nest.

There! It is unmistakeably

some large bird.
Cameracamera! zoomclickswiff,
I trap it in a twelve-pixel
speckle, bundle it

into my sack, wings
elbow ribs, black screech
eyes, livid stripes, yellow
meat hooks, a fairground
prize only desired for
right now, and why not?

Somewhere an ornithologist
dreams hours in his hide,
and curled, shivering at his feet,
my giant otter.

Night Walk

'For this activity you will need . . .'

Flash light to make mirrors
of their eyes, silver on bugs, red
on black cayman, to watch them watching.

> *Quinoa in your belly;*
> *a careful footstep;*
> *two black cats to bookend the night.*

Bug spray for the female mosquito,
her lifetime of fevers, for the sandfly,
his patient, chronic sores.

> *Plantain on your tongue;*
> *ears tuned to chorus;*
> *a katydid at your right shoulder.*

Camera to catch them: spider,
snake, tree frog, walking stick,
a highway of leaf cutters.

> *Sugar-rough brazil nuts in your pocket;*
> *eyes wide as black full moons;*
> *oil-green beetle like a brooch on your collar.*

Poncho – beneath the canopy
it rains long after
the sky has emptied.

Pisco on your breath;
dreams already hatching;
a black bee heavy on each eyelid.

Two
dogs going
at it in the street
like, well, two dogs
in the street. This is
the moment of
creation at its
unsurpassed
best. It is the
crass undoing
of mankind's
close selection,
the fumbling
open of corset
laces by sweaty
stableboy hands.
This unaesthetic
pairing of shaggy
carpetbag with sleek
prize dachshund is one big
doggie hard-on stuck up at human
efforts. His face is two glazed eyes, is
absent and laughing, hers is eyes also,
rolling doubtful chestnuts, brown in
white. Wide around twin stings
of need   of guilt.

PROHIBIDO
EL
PASO

The skull is surely grinning for a reason.
The lettering on his sign is bold, red,
hand-rendered in what is probably not blood.

He is pleased with the crusty bubbled paint.
It gives him an aged authority;
gives his comical pinprick eyes,
triangle nose hole, knitting needle crossbones
their classic horror flick feel. All he wants
is a brisk breeze from through the Andes
to send him pivoting like a stiff flag,
creaking back and forth on his post.

You know enough Spanish and I
enough about pictures of skulls to turn back.

When we stood there together moments ago
he was doing his job so well – no man
would have disobeyed, considered descending
the narrow path built up against the cliff,
too far from the top, too far from the bottom
for comfort, down towards his 'bridge',
two planks that cross a twenty-foot wide
gap in the path. No man, despite
the detailed placard on its renovation.

But now, returned, alone with him,
I forget what it was I had forgotten.

I think what it would be to shuffle to the bridge,
shoulder blades scraping the hot cliff face,
to court the one-thousand-nine-hundred foot drop,
my toes playing air piano at its edge,
to stare giddied at the vast possibility
of the landscape below, tickled by specks
and threads of life, to be lassoed by vertigo
and lean far enough to allow perhaps a slip –

and I see that the skull's grin is merely
expressing the chivalry appropriate
to an inappropriate invitation.

Cochineal

Someone has been here with icing sugar!
This spoony cactus limb is blistered
by a cluster of bodies:
a comfort of females.

Each is the size of a beauty spot, heavy
as silver. Pinched,
she disappears, leaving only
blood-bright confection.

       In the sunshine-hot Cortina,
       red Smarties; carmine bleeding
       into my fingerprints.

Machu Picchu

No, the present has not fallen from my eyes like tumbling granite; my head is not overflowing with memory, juices running from a macheted fruit. My feet have never trodden your steps, my hands do not know the curves of your altars. I cannot read the date in the Intihuatana. My heart syncopates, but not from recognition; my eyes are bright, but not with the light of the past. Your ghost will not stand up inside me, will not spring a feathered cloak from my shoulders, will not guide me to my throne.

You are a stranger. You are a stranger to me. Yet all the way to the Inca bridge you follow me, half way to the Sun Gate, through every room, chasing lizards, talking to birds. I seek you in the shade of the Watchman's Hut, on the steep paths between roofless houses, peering deep beneath the Torreon. You spy me through impossible gaps in the ashlar stonework, hover hands over my shoulders as I look out to vertigo. I feel the wake of air where you have rounded a corner, paused at the Condor's Eye, slipped beneath its outstretched wing.

So, I did not bring you with me, but can I have you now? Now, cut in insistent sunlight, your sloping walls, your squat bromeliads, your mortality-raising trails. Can I have you: your orchids, your dead quarry, your trapezoid windows? Can I have you: your temples, your zipping hummingbirds, your faultlines? I want you: your puzzle-board blueprints, your break-neck terraces, your sky. I want you: your tragedy, your jungle grave, your guessworked past.

Yana Phuyu

Yana Phuyu means 'dark clouds' in Quechua; it is the collective name for the Pachatira, dark cloud constellations within Mayu (the Milky Way) as seen from the Southern Hemisphere. The shapes of the Pachatira are seen in Quechuan culture as the shadows of animals that have come to drink from the river of the Milky Way.

He explains that we see it all wrong,
that the creatures we have drawn
dot-to-dot all about the universe
are the hand-me-downs
of men wedded to the straight line;

that we have been seeing it all backwards,
white on black – I mean who
draws white on black, aside from tailors
with their toothy chalk wheels,
teachers drawing more straight lines?

So, the stars I have left behind
are not real here – there is no hunter
to protect me at night, no steady
plough share to lean on, my lion
is not a lion, I am not a lion –

He points to Mayu, the milky river
that flows above us. One-by-one
as my eyes fill, they come to drink,
darkening its waters with their shadows,
the Yana Phuyu, each Pachatira

a spill of fluid night – Mach'acuay
the serpent, Hanp'atu – toad, Yacana
– the llama and her calf. At her fetlocks,
Atoq – the fox – I see his red eyes,
align them with my own, blink, see.

A
T
O
K

A
T
O
K

In Quechuan culture Atoq, the fox, is one of the animals that comes each night to drink from the Milky Way (Mayu) as seen from the Southern Hemisphere. The animals appear as dark shadows against the white river Mayu.

Like a telephone ringing in two rooms, there is your name, sprayed on twin bridge supports. Atok? Atoq? My Atoq? The train carries me on, your double-naming fixed before me as if it had been written in light.

My fox, are you lost? Did you follow me home across the sky, slinking eighteen paces back, ducking behind satellite dustbins, pausing at the lit doorways of stars, a shy stray? What have I done?

Did you follow me only to baulk at the front door's creak, the face of our black cat, shadow-puppet sharp on the hall's lit screen? Did the snap of the door latch cut your star strings? Did you not know the way back?

No, you did not – how could you? And so your misplaced paws took you, sliced in and out of existence by street light, to Egham station where the wet tracks shone like Mayu under the moon. And you followed them.

When the boys found you, you took up their shape, hooded, nocturnal, began again, let slip from your mind the slick temptation of the llama's hock, marked out a new Mayu across the damp brick of the rail networks.

And this is where you exist now – only the places you have sprayed. You are just four letters with a changing date – '09, '10, '11, '12, pulling away in time and space, your white absence setting in the Southern sky, a skin on cooling milk.